contents

the business of clothes

The British clothing industry not only produces a wide variety of **outputs** – clothes of all shapes and sizes for males and females of all ages – but also involves a wide range of company types. The significance of clothing manufacture in British industry is likely to remain for some time to come. However, like many areas of manufacture, it has had to face change in recent years. This change has been as much a result of developments in the fashion world as technological advances.

Clothing manufacturers may be very small scale, producing a low volume for a limited **market** and employing only the minimum of staff. At the other extreme, companies may have a huge output with a large market, and employ thousands of workers.

Street fashion

Couture garments are those produced by the couture fashion **houses**. They are of a high quality, made in small quantities at a very high cost. Traditionally they have always set the trend as far as fashion is concerned. Yet in recent years the dominance of these fashion houses has been in decline. This is partly due to a more relaxed approach to fashion. People are choosing to wear clothes they feel comfortable in rather than those that are regarded by others as being 'fashionable'. Multicultural British society is no longer prepared to have its hemline dictated by designers. Street fashion is now a strong feature of today's clothing industry.

Street fashion can be seen in most high street stores, where the consumer sector is no longer exclusively female. It is an example of affordable fashion for the mass population. It is marketed at young people who are likely to want something new in a few weeks' time. These clothes are not meant to have a particularly long life, so their price tag is usually a moderate one. Street fashion has been made possible by the wider range of cheaper fabrics available and faster production methods due to technological advances.

This means that the selling and making of clothes is dictated by the consumer, rather than by designers. The clothing

Street fashion is affordable fashion marketed mainly at young people.

industry has had to adapt in order to be more versatile and flexible. Now production runs may be short because a different style is likely to be required very quickly.

Staple garments

In complete contrast to the fast turnover of street fashions, another sector of today's clothing market manufactures staple garments. These are clothes that are not greatly influenced by fashion and might include schoolwear, shirts and underwear. Consumers demand staple garments regularly and in large numbers. It is not uncommon today for an adult to own twenty pairs of briefs whereas in the 1940s or 1950s, three or four pairs would have been acceptable. Consequently, companies producing these garments are able to set their production processes to run for months, or even years, without a great deal of alteration in style.

Mass market

Somewhere between the street fashions and staple garments lie the clothes produced in their hundreds or thousands for the **mass market**. These are the dresses, suits, leisure and sportswear that consumers frequently demand but only if they are both fashionable and well made. When these garments are produced, the level of change in style between each batch varies according to the current trends and the type of garment. A dress may alter quite radically in shape whereas a suit may just have minor adjustments to the collar or line of the trousers. This type of clothing manufacture must be able to cope with

▼ *Staple garments include schoolwear.*

continual changes as a result of new **product development**. Research to find out what consumers want and need produces new products all the time. These new products may require a different colour, fabric, shape, feature or size from the previous production batch. Competition from other manufacturers means companies must meet market opportunities as soon as they arise.

clothes and the consumer

Consumer satisfaction

The main aim of the clothing industry is to provide garments that consumers want to buy. A garment must satisfy all of a consumer's needs. When someone looks at a garment in a shop, they often focus first on the colour, fabric design and shape of the garment. Together, these aspects provide an immediate visual image. They are the basis for whether or not the garment is appealing. If it does appeal, trying it on may be the next step, and then other considerations come into play – for example, how well it fits, how comfortable it is, when and where it can be worn, what it goes with, its brand name, how it can be washed and, of course, its price.

Naturally the considerations which are most important will depend on the type of garment and on the individual consumer. If someone is happy with the garment and purchases it, the manufacturer has successfully satisfied the consumer's needs.

▼ *When browsing in a clothes shop you are likely to focus on the colour, fabric design and shape of the garment.*

Retailer satisfaction

Of course, the clothing industry cannot survive just by pleasing its customers. It must also make a profit. This is essential because without a profit a business cannot survive. As long as the consumer is content that the product they have bought is good value for money, then everyone in the process of making, selling and buying is content. However, this success is largely dependent on good **marketing**. Marketing is the way in which a manufacturer or retailer **promotes** their product. This is done in a variety of ways, including the use of advertising and effective packaging and display of goods.

Marketing department

Large clothing manufacturers will have a marketing department. If not, a company will employ a manager who is responsible for the marketing of the clothes produced. The marketing manager or department has three main areas of responsibility: marketing, merchandising and sales.

Marketing

One aspect of marketing is **market research**, which aims to establish **perceived consumer need**, that is to find out what consumers want and need. When carrying out market research it is possible to identify a gap in the market. This occurs when consumers want, but currently cannot buy, a particular item. When marketing reveals a gap or 'niche', this is known as niche marketing. As long as there is sufficient demand and it is possible to make the item at a profit, then a manufacturer can fill the gap or niche.

Athletes can publicize a company's name and logo.

As well as identifying gaps in the market, marketing involves promoting existing goods. This is so that consumers not only get the type of products they want, but are aware of the products on sale.

Merchandising

Merchandising is concerned with **product development**. Once a product is on the market it is unlikely to sell at the same rate all the time. There will be a greater demand for certain products at certain times, such as swimwear in the summer. However, not all adjustments can be anticipated so easily. A fashion fad may really take off, and the manufacturer will be suddenly inundated with orders. Merchandising involves giving certain goods priority in production as the demand changes.

Sales

Sales are also the responsibility of the marketing department, but this time the retailer is the customer. Manufacturers must sell their products to retailers who in turn sell them to consumers. It is up to the marketing team to inform retailers about any new items the company is making and to predict the retailers' response so they are able to deliver the new stock quickly.

Promoting goods

All sales promotion, whether it is aimed at the public or retailers, is based on effective communication. Communication is important because it can get a company's name and image established, which should lead to increased sales. Promotion can be carried out through:

- advertising in newspapers, magazines, films or on posters, radio, television and the Internet
- publicity from other people – this might be when famous people wear particular clothes, perhaps with a logo or designer label
- personal selling – people buying expensive clothes may be given personal attention but otherwise personal selling is likely to occur when manufacturers are demonstrating their latest range to potential **clients** (retailers)
- presentations such as fashion shows – these are probably the most visual and effective way to promote clothes; they are held regularly by designers and manufacturers but retailers occasionally put on fashion shows for their customers, usually those who have a store card or account.

a design process

Consumer needs

It is essential that retailers understand the needs of their consumers, particularly if they are selling to the **mass market**. To do this, retailers must keep track of selling patterns in their stores. Most major retailers now work on a worldwide scale. This gives them greater awareness of what is new and selling well in the major capital cities, which helps them to predict trends in the mass market. Retailers must also keep up to date with fashion trends, and with fabric, **yarn** and **component** developments. By doing all this, they can give guidance to their fabric and garment suppliers about predicted consumer needs for the forthcoming season.

Garment designers

As well as receiving advice from retailers, the garment designers must themselves stay on top of fashion trends. They also need to know the manufacturer's production requirements and what the manufacturing plant is capable of producing. This way they can offer designs that can be realistically produced and satisfy the **perceived consumer need**.

This process is not as easy as it sounds. Change happens quickly in fashion, and design ideas are constantly being proposed, discussed and modified. A contract for a series of garments cannot be confirmed until the type, colour and design of fabric, trimmings, silhouette and cost have all been decided. Even after all this, the garments continue to be developed as the technical aspects of fit, **grading**, construction and **garment performance** are considered.

▲ *A garment designer will modify a garment during the design process.*

Design processes

The processes of garment design can be divided into four stages.

1 Design initiation – the first stage is to assess consumer needs and use them to determine colour, silhouette, style and fabric design.
2 Design concept – at this stage many design options are explored. Designs that satisfy perceived consumer needs are produced as design offers.
3 Decision-making process – design offers are considered and used to develop a range of designs. Decisions are made about the choice of designs, fabric, trimmings etc.
4 Technical design – finally, the design offer that has been accepted must be refined so that it precisely fulfills the fit, construction, garment performance and production requirements.

Design research

There are various types of research that need to be carried out during the process of designing and making garments. Initially, **market research** is needed to find out what consumers like and don't like. Designers also need to carry out research to help them with their ideas. They may need to develop a **mood board**, which will involve researching colour schemes, fabric types, images, consumer preferences and so on. Once sufficient research has been carried out, designers can begin to sketch their ideas and perhaps make a **prototype**.

A prototype is a model of an idea. It is made to see how well the idea works. In clothes design a prototype is important to ensure the pattern pieces fit together correctly and the garment has the right look or image. Prototypes of garments are often referred to as **toiles**. Toiles are usually made out of calico or a similar, cheap fabric. Initially, a toile might be put on a mannequin, which is a wooden or plastic human dummy. The mannequin's size can be altered slightly but a model (or the **client**) would need to try on the toile to ensure an exact fit.

You need to make a prototype of a pattern as well, particularly if the design is complex. The pattern pieces are pinned or stuck to represent the way the item will be joined. Although paper does not hang in the same way as fabric, it is more economical to test and alter a paper pattern than to find you need to make alterations after the fabric has been cut.

When designing new products a mood board can be used to capture a feeling or express a theme.

Sample clothes

The prototype pattern is used to make a sample garment. This process is carried out by a skilled machinist, who works out how best to join the pieces together. After the sample garments are completed and the production process has been established, the production costs can be predicted. Quality and performance checks are then carried out on the garments, and pattern pieces are produced. These are used for the **grading** and **marker planning** processes.

Finally, a **product specification** can be written. This contains precise details about the garment so that it can be reproduced on a large scale.

clothing manufacture

No matter how large or small a clothing manufacturer, the production process will involve more or less the same stages:

1 Cutting – this includes a variety of procedures being carried out in order to turn fabrics and other **components** into cut garments.

2 Sewing – this is when garments are assembled. Cut garments are sewn and under-pressed and quality checks take place. Other operations such as embroidery or pleating may be done at this stage or they may be completed by an **outside contractor**.

3 Pressing – the final or top pressing takes place.

4 Finishing – the stage at which labels and tags for hanging a garment are attached.

5 Final inspection – when garments, or a selection of them, are inspected before being packaged.

6 Packing – the final stage, when garments are either hung or folded and then bagged or boxed, depending on the type of garment and retail outlet.

▲ *Highly fashionable items have a short life span.*

Demanding fashion

Over the last thirty years or so, changes in fashion have been both dramatic and frequent. This has caused problems for those who make clothes. While they need to meet consumer demand, they are also limited by their existing manufacturing facilities. However, the clothing industry has gradually been able to organize itself so that it can produce garments efficiently and quickly. Although there are variations within companies, the main aspects of the British clothing industry are outlined here.

Types of clothing

Within the industry 'clothes' generally refer to garments worn on the body, so the following information excludes accessories such as hats, gloves, socks, shoes etc. A clothing manufacturer may specialize in one type of garment or a range of garments, and these can be divided up as follows:

- blouses
- casual clothing and sportswear
- children's wear
- dresses
- knitwear
- women's tailored outerwear
- lingerie and pyjamas
- men's tailored outerwear
- shirts
- underwear
- waterproof outerwear
- workwear and uniforms.

It remains to be seen how these sectors will alter in the future as more clothes become unisex.

You can also classify each of these clothing types according to their style variation and frequency. Style variation is the degree to which a basic garment varies in design, fabric and assembly from one fashion to the next. Frequency refers to the speed or rate at which the style variation occurs. So, fashion may cause a blouse to alter slightly and slowly whereas a skirt may change dramatically in style, and do so very quickly.

Types of production

Not all types of manufacture are suitable for all types of garment. A production run is the length of time for which one garment type will be produced. The length of the production run will have an effect on all other aspects of manufacture, such as the size of the factory or unit.

The length of production run depends on the type of garment being made:
• Staple garments – these are produced continuously and only require minor changes in colour, cut and fabric, so

their manufacture is relatively straightforward. Examples include underwear and workclothes such as overalls.
• Semi-styled products – garments that are also mass produced but require more frequent changes in style, such as men's shirts. The fabric and style may alter quite frequently so production runs are shorter than staple garments.
• Clothes that frequently alter in style include women's skirts and dresses. These are styled products and production runs have to be short to allow for considerable changes in fabric, colour and design.
• Highly fashionable items have a short lifespan. They are produced very quickly and in very short runs. Each style may be totally unique in shape, colour and design. These are known as fashion products.

The bar charts below show how different types of garment production affect other aspects of manufacturing.

▼ The length of production run will depend on the type of garment being made. Compare the production run of the garments shown here.

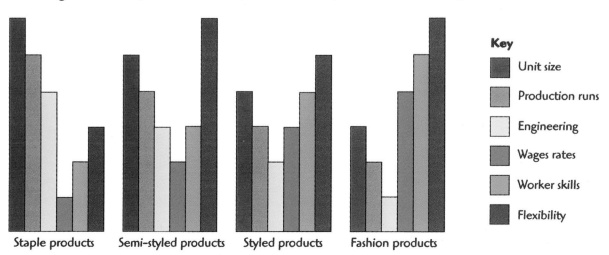

Key
■ Unit size
■ Production runs
□ Engineering
■ Wages rates
■ Worker skills
■ Flexibility

Staple products   Semi-styled products   Styled products   Fashion products

S.R. Gent

S.R. Gent (UK) Ltd is a clothing manufacturer based in South Yorkshire. It currently produces garments for Marks & Spencer. Their Rotherham factory assembles a wide variety of items, from nighties to leggings. All the clothes start and finish at the main depot in Barnsley.

Cutwork loading bay

When a delivery of cut garments arrives at S.R. Gents, they are stored in the cutwork loading bays. Each bag or 'lay' contains several dozen cut garments. A card system is used to record the contents with their style number and the bay in which they are stored. When the cut garments are collected, they must be taken from the correct lay to ensure that the colour of the various pieces matches exactly.

Once the sorters are ready for the next batch of garments they are taken from the cutwork loading bay to the sorting area. Here they are sorted and placed on appropriate trolleys. S.R. Gent uses two assembly systems, the conventional or 'sit-down' system and the 'stand-up' system. A different type of trolley is used for each system. The trolley contains everything necessary to make up the garment. The sorters also print tickets to identify the finished articles.

An example of a 'stand-up' assembly system. ▶

Method sheet

No matter which system is used, all machinists must follow a precise method for constructing a garment. When a new item of clothing is introduced, a method sheet arrives from Barnsley. First, the manager makes up the item, then the supervisor and finally the machinists are shown how to assemble it.

The method sheet contains every single detail in the construction, the order in which it is to be carried out and the time taken for that task. These 'time values' are very important because the factory uses a piece-work system. This means the machinists are paid for each 'piece' or item they complete rather than the number of hours they work.

Checking and pressing

When a garment is complete, including labellings (see page 35), it is inspected in the 'pre-exam' area. Some garments then go through the steam tunnel before being pressed while others go straight to the pressers. The pressers work with irons

that are automatically fed water for steaming. They also use a suction system operated with a foot pedal. The garment is placed on the ironing board and held in place with suction while it is being pressed. After being counted and bagged, all clothes are loaded into the loading bay to await collection by the van from Barnsley. There they are stored in the warehouse ready for dispatch to Marks & Spencer's various retail outlets.

Tarzan pyjamas

These pyjamas are made using S.R. Gent's 'stand-up' assembly system. Four machinists make up the team and they each carry out a series of tasks and pass the garment on to the next worker.

Machinist 1:
- Begins by machining the front and back 'rise' (centre seams) on the pyjama bottoms using an **overlocker**; also stitches the label into the back seam at the same time.
- Measures a length of flat elastic and places it on the next machine where it is inserted and sewn into the waist.
- Stitches the leg ends using a twin-needle machine.
- Sews the inside leg seams in one go using an overlocker.
- Passes garment to Machinist 2.

Machinist 2:
- Completes the assembly of the pyjama bottoms using a **backlatch machine** which finishes off the ends of cotton. (Continues tasks with pyjama bottoms over his or her shoulder to ensure pyjama pairs are constructed in one go.)
- Reinforces one shoulder of the top by sewing in a special tape.
- Adds a ribbed edge to the neck.
- Reinforces the second shoulder of the top as before.
- Passes garments (top and bottoms) to Machinist 3.

Machinist 3:
- Stitches the sleeve ends using a twin-needle machine.
- Collects the front of the top from a trolley on which a stack of decorated tops are waiting.
- Attaches one sleeve to the body of the top using the overlocker.
- Attaches the second sleeve in the same way.
- Passes garments on to Machinist 4.

Machinist 4:
- Stitches one side seam.
- Stitches the second side seam and incorporates a label into the seam.
- Twin-stitches the top's hem.
- Hangs the completed garment on a rail ready for the next step in the finishing process.

▲ The finished garment.

clothing technology

There are many different systems used in the clothing industry to produce garments or **outputs**. The type of approach used by a manufacturer will depend on the nature of the clothes and the size of the organization. A production system may be totally manual, where everything is done by hand, or totally automated, where everything is done by machine. However, most systems use a combination of these methods.

'Making through'

'Making through' is a traditional method of clothing manufacture. In this system a garment is made from start to finish by the same person. The operator is given a bundle of cut items which he or she then assembles using hand and machine stitching. The operator must be highly skilled as well as versatile. This is a **labour-intensive** method of manufacture and therefore the clothes are expensive. However, it is regarded as the most rewarding of the systems of manufacture as it is less repetitive for the worker and gives them a sense of ownership of the final garment. Today, **bespoke** clothing might use the making through production method.

Section system

When making clothes using the section system, operators specialize in the assembly of one part of a garment. They do all the tasks required to complete that section or **component** of the finished article.

Progressive bundles

In the progressive bundle system of manufacture, clothes are assembled

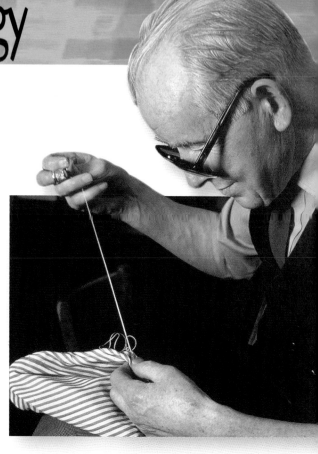

▲ Bespoke tailoring is an example of the 'making through' production method.

gradually. As the name implies, they are put together as they progress through the system. Each section of work has a store at either side so completed work from the previous stage can be stored ready for one set of operators while their work is stored for the next series of operators. This system is versatile and efficient and is used for large-scale production.

Straight line system

The straight line system is also used when large quantities of clothing are being manufactured. Tasks are organized according to the time they take to complete rather than the order in which the garments are put together. This means the success of the system is based on efficient timing.

14

Conveyor belts

Conveyor belts have been used for many years in the clothing industry to transport garments, or parts of garments, from operator to operator. However, today's computerized systems of feeding and controlling production have led to a faster and more efficient industry. Operators are positioned at work stations and the selective conveyor belt system automatically feeds the operator with work and takes completed items to the next stage or operator.

UPS

The UPS (unit production system) uses computers to plan, control and direct the flow of work through a system. A unit of production is a whole garment (rather than a bundle) which is automatically taken from work station to work station. The flow of production has already been decided and the computer is set accordingly. Each garment component is brought as close to the operator as possible. This reduces the amount of movement required by the operator to grab and position the next item to be stitched. This type of computerized system is likely to be found in the mass production of clothes. It is expensive but it has the advantage of being able to respond quickly to changes in fashion.

Quick response

The quick response sewing system was first developed in Japan. It is important because it allows manufacturing adjustments to be made quickly as the **market** changes. Each work station has two to four machines and one operator takes a garment through the necessary tasks, including pressing, before it is passed on to the next work station. All the components of a garment are loaded on to a hanging clamp attached to a trolley. This is then transported by a computer-controlled overhead trolley system, rather than a conveyor belt. Each work station is kept informed about the style of garment being worked on via the computerized trolley.

The GERBERmover GM-300 is a fully computerized unit production system. It uses an overhead conveyor to transport products from work station to work station, one product at a time. Operations can even be performed without removing parts from the hanger.

one-off production

When products are made specifically for a consumer or **client**, the production method is known as one-off production. This means one garment or outfit has been made either by one person or by a group of people, each using their particular area of expertise. It would be made to suit and fit that person; it would be a unique accessory. Equally, a consumer can choose a garment from a range in a shop and then have that garment made-to-measure. Although someone else may have the same style of clothing, the consumer has one that has been made to fit perfectly.

Bespoke tailoring

This is the name given to the production of custom-made clothes. Traditionally all clothes were made by hand for individual customers because there was no such thing as mass production. Today suits are often made this way, particularly for men. The suit is still the traditional outfit for many jobs. As they are worn every day, it is important that they fit well and are comfortable. The customer chooses a particular style of suit and the type of fabric. Measurements are taken initially and during production the customer will have a fitting so the tailor can make any necessary adjustments. Such custom-made clothes are expensive because production is time-consuming and **labour-intensive**.

Another way to have clothes that fit perfectly is to buy from shops that offer an alteration service. Although less expensive than bespoke tailoring it is an additional cost to the price of the outfit. You put the

An example of haute couture.

garment on, and a tailor or seamstress notes any adjustments that need to be made. You collect the altered clothes when they are ready. This is usually offered in shops that sell wedding dresses or suits.

Haute couture

As a method of production, **haute couture** is time-consuming, expensive and labour-intensive. It requires a high level of skill from everyone involved in the garment's manufacture. The number of consumers who wear these clothes is tiny; it is thought that there are only about 2000 women in the world who can afford haute couture. Yet, it continues to exist as an exclusive sector of the clothing industry.

Designer houses

When a designer sets up their own fashion **house**, they really have made it in the fashion world. It is within the walls of couture houses that designers unleash their wildest fashion ideas; designing couture clothes provides them with the licence to be truly creative. Many big designer names allow their houses to go on even after their death, enabling talented designers to continue their fashionable innovations. The couture houses of Chanel and Christian Dior, for example, live on under the guise of other designers.

Couture survives, despite the outrageous price tags, because the elaborate designs of the famous catwalks eventually end up as ready-to-wear collections and then high street fashions. They also survive thanks to their money-spinning off-shoots such as perfumes, handbags and other accessories.

Quality counts

Couture clothes are the ultimate in luxury. They require creative designers and workers with the highest expertise in textile manipulation. These people then have the choice of the most opulent fabrics and the most lavish embellishments; delicate embroidery silks, mother of pearl buttons, bird of paradise feathers, glittering glass beads, usually by the thousand and always hand sewn. If a couture designer wants something for their collection then even if it means finding a supplier from the other side of the world, find it they will. Leading milliners, jewellers and shoe designers are brought in to complete the ensemble which may take weeks or months to complete. Haute couture is the most costly and the least cost-effective area of the clothing industry.

Couture today

Contemporary couture designers include Alexander McQueen for Givenchy, John Galliano for Christian Dior, Karl Lagerfeld for Chanel, Emanuel Ungaro, Jean Paul Gaultier and Christian Lacroix. Some will also have ready-to-wear collections while others are exclusively couture.

Couture outfits are owned by a tiny proportion of the population due to the prohibitively high price tags. However, if you are a very tall size eight, you could buy one a few thousand pounds cheaper from a shop selling models' sample clothes!

clothes to treasure – a case study

Jemima Khan

Jemima Khan's **couture** dresses retail at around £800 each. They are also in big demand. The reason for their popularity is that each dress has been hand-crafted using **labour-intensive** embroidery stitches. No two dresses are the same and they can take between four and six months to complete. What is more, although they are made in England, they are then shipped over to Pakistan to be embellished.

The business

The inspiration for Jemima Khan's business came from her own desire to create an appreciation in the West for Pakistan's exquisite hand embroidery. She quite rightly predicted there would be a **market** for her collection of silk dresses, decorated with embroidery and beading. She also wanted to help maintain the traditional crafts of Pakistan. These are now in danger of dying out due to more cost-effective and less time-consuming methods of machine embroidery.

The proceeds

A further motivation for setting up her exclusive business was to raise funds for the only cancer hospital in Pakistan. The Shaukat Khanum Memorial Cancer Hospital and Research Centre is maintained by Imran Khan. He had the hospital built in memory of his mother. The hospital treats 90 per cent of its patients for free and needs about £4 million a year to run. Consequently, Jemima spends a great deal of her time fundraising in addition to giving all the profits from her fashion business to the hospital.

The production

Jemima Khan designs all the garments in her collection, although her passion lies with the intricate detail of the embroidery rather than the actual design of the clothes. The style of each dress is often simple in order to display the decoration to its full advantage. Each one is unique because even where the cut might be the same, the colours, trimmings and embroidery are always different.

Her clothes are made from pure silk fabrics that are cut and sewn in England using standards equivalent to couture clothing. They are then transported to Pakistan where each garment is individually stamped by hand using a wooden block. There are about a thousand different blocks to choose from, each one having been carved with a traditional design or motif. The blocks are stained using a henna dye which gently transfers the pattern on to the fabric.

The garments are then taken to the villages within Pakistan where highly talented local women begin the elaborate embroidery process. They work from home using miniature frames to hold the fabric in place while they create minute stitches. Their embroidery skills have been passed down to them through the generations.

As their homes are often not much more than a mud hut, this basic working environment means there is a risk that an expensive silk dress may become damaged. However, Jemima manages to keep track of up to a thousand dresses at a time.

Some examples from Jemima Khan's collection of silk dresses. Each one is exquisitely hand embroidered in Pakistan.

Every woman works on a dress for twelve hours a day, stitching the eye-strainingly small stitches by hand. In the western world, work that requires such painstaking dedication is rare, and it is likely that it will die out eventually in developing countries such as Pakistan. For this reason Jemima Khan is intent on maintaining the art for as long as possible. Hopefully her dresses will be preserved by their owners as items to treasure.

The embroidery

The embroidery sewn by those employed by Jemima Khan is known as Chikan-Kari. This four-hundred-year-old tradition originated in Persia (modern Iran) and took its inspiration from lace. It was brought to Pakistan by the Moghul princess Mehr-Un-Nisa, and its development has continued ever since. Each garment takes months to complete because more than a hundred different types of stitch may be used in a single design.

The future

Jemima Khan's collection is currently supplied to ten shops around the world. However, she is now considering cutting back on production in order to produce her quality garments at a more moderate pace. Consumers will then be able to buy her clothes from her London studio or by special delivery. Her original idea for a 'hobby' has grown into a highly successful business venture and Jemima Khan wants to maintain that success but on a limited scale.

designer labels

Designer labels are clothes that have the status of being associated with a designer's name. The designer may not have designed the garment personally – it may have been created by someone from their design team – but it still carries the designer label. Some consumers prefer to look for specific designer clothes not just because they want to be seen wearing a particular label, but because the clothes are a good fit or they particularly like the cut. Designerwear can be relatively expensive because you are paying for the name as well as the garment. Examples include French Connection, Nicole Farhi and Christa Davies.

▲ These are a few of the shops that sell designer labels.

Copycat designers

Recently there has been a lot of controversy about clothes made by copycat designers. In fact, although these are sold as designer labels, they are an imitation of the real thing. Obviously this means both the consumer and the original designer are losing out. Just as there are laws of copyright protecting people against having their writing copied, there are laws protecting designers against 'copycats'. A designer can protect their work by signing and dating their original drawings. This will prove the work is theirs and if anyone produces exactly the same garment then they are breaking copyright law. It is important that original sketches are kept because the actual clothes are not copyright, just the drawings. A finished design can be dated and registered with a bank or solicitor to prove it is the designer's own work.

Patents

If a designer has created a garment using a new process or has incorporated a totally new idea into the design, they can then apply for a **patent**. This prevents another company or person from copying the design for a specified length of time. A patent will only be granted if the product is genuinely original. If necessary, an international patent can be obtained so the product cannot be copied abroad. In textiles, products most likely to require a patent include new fibres, new machinery and equipment used during the processing of fibres and fabrics.

Second to none

Today it is possible to buy perfectly legitimate designer labels but without paying top prices. Buying from secondhand shops has not only become acceptable, it is also a trendy way to buy your clothes. It is environmentally sound as well because clothes are being 'recycled' rather than thrown away. Often you are supporting a worthwhile charitable cause, too. As an added bonus, when you buy from a secondhand shop, it is unlikely you will see anyone else wearing the same outfit as you! The trend towards buying from secondhand stores is probably also linked to a more relaxed attitude to fashion. Mixing and matching clothes from different eras is all part of the versatile mix of styles characteristic of today's fashion.

Some secondhand stores actually specialize in designerwear. There are plenty of people who will discard their designer jacket because it was from the previous season and there are many more people happy to wear it if it can be bought at a reasonable price.

Designer jeans

It is thought that the first designer's name to appear on a pair of jeans was that of Gloria Vanderbilt. At a time when many designers still regarded denim jeans as workwear rather than items of fashion, the president of an American manufacturing company, Warren Hirsh, had the idea of producing designer label clothes for the **mass market**. He decided to start with jeans and, as he had a team of professional designers, all he needed was someone to put their famous name to the denims. Eventually he found Gloria Vanderbilt, an heiress who had begun selling her own line of home furnishings. Her signature appeared above a picture of a swan on the back hip pocket of the jeans.

As Warren Hirsh had experience in **marketing** he decided it would be a good idea for Gloria Vanderbilt to model and advertise the jeans herself. He was hoping they would then appeal to more mature, **suburban** women and he was right because very soon, well-dressed women everywhere were wearing Vanderbilt jeans.

Gloria Vanderbilt jeans are thought to be the first items of designer label clothes produced for the mass market. ▶

the cost of clothes

Anyone involved in making and selling clothes is also in the business of making money. Profits are important so money can be ploughed back to improve and expand the business. Profits make for a secure business and give security to the workers. Whether or not a profit is achieved is largely dependent on whether or not consumers buy the garments on offer. However, long before clothes go on sale, careful costings must be worked out to ensure the price is acceptable for both the consumer and the manufacturer.

Long before clothes go on sale, costings must be calculated. The price of a garment must be acceptable to both the consumer and the manufacturers.

Counting the cost

The costing of a garment is usually prepared by a manufacturer's finance department. Once prepared, the costing sheet will be presented to the management for approval. The cost of a new garment must be looked at in relation to all other costs. If an item of clothing is predicted to be in high demand but the production costs are very expensive, it may not be possible to produce it. The ultimate decision will be taken by the management.

The finance department gather their information about costing from a variety of sources. The cutting room or **marker planning** area will provide details about the amount and type of fabric and any trimmings needed. The purchasing department will know how much the fabric and trimmings cost. The production area will be able to supply information such as the time and costs involved in cutting, sewing and finishing the garment. The more **components** in

a garment and the more operations required during production, the more it will cost to make. The number of workers involved and the amount of different machines needed will also affect the cost.

Costing sheet

Once the finance department have all the necessary information, they can start to complete a costing sheet. This will show details of the costings for:
• materials
• labour
• overheads
• other expenses, including value-added tax (VAT).

Overheads are the additional costs involved in making the garments. Fixed overheads are the costs that have to be paid and will not vary according to type of product being made. These would include, for example, rent of buildings, rates payable to the local authority and insurance of property and equipment. Variable overheads are those that depend on the amount and type of garments being produced. They might include energy, administration costs and maintainance costs. The finance department must work out all the overheads when they prepare a costing sheet.

The price is right

When all costs are added together, the result is the total cost price of the garment. This is used to decide whether it can be sold at a profit. In other words, whether the price consumers are willing to pay is greater than the total cost of making the garment. Costing sheets are used to determine the selling price and the profit for the company. The amount of profit added can be anything from 10 per cent to 100 per cent, depending on the type of clothing.

Price brackets

Many large retailers use a system of **price bracketing**. This means items of clothing are categorized and given a price range. The retailer will only buy manufacturer's products that fit into their price brackets. For example, a retailer may use the following price brackets for female knitwear:

- Bargain £8 – £12
- Cheap £15 – £20
- Average £21 – £35
- Expensive £40 – £60
- Luxury £65 – £80

A manufacturer will know that the retailer's product buyer will only choose goods that fit into their price brackets. This means they must cost their garments very carefully. The amount of profit added will depend on the amount of risk involved in the sale. A **fad** fashion is a high-risk item because consumers are likely to want it for only a short time. Consequently, the price bracket of a fad fashion will be wider than that of a 'safe' garment that the manufacturer knows will sell well.

The female knitwear shown here might fall into a wide price bracket because it is regarded as a fad fashion item. ▶

computers and clothes

CAD

Computers can be used from the very beginning of the design stage through manufacturing and **marketing**, to the sale of garments. Computer-aided design (CAD) has enabled designers to produce exciting new fabrics easily and efficiently, but there are arguments about how creative a designer can be, sitting at a computer screen. Some people claim that computers, by their very nature, cannot be creative because their calculations are based on computing information. However, as a tool, CAD can certainly be used to produce original and creative clothes. Textile designers can apply sophisticated techniques to reproduce computerized effects on to fabric which are then used by fashion designers.

Fast fashions

CAD certainly speeds up the process of design and also makes certain processes less tedious. For example, colour schemes can be altered with the click of a button, rather than having to re-do the entire design. Even though designs for clothes are computer-generated, they are still as unique as those sketched by hand because every designer will have their own way of using a computer. Also, CAD is frequently combined with freehand drawing; using one does not exclude the use of the other.

CAM

Computer-aided manufacture (CAM) is now an important feature of the clothing industry. CAM is a process of making a product using equipment that is controlled by a computer. Large companies are likely to use computers to control their entire manufacturing process. Some of the ways in which computers are used in the clothing industry are outlined below.

Pattern design

Traditionally all patterns were produced by manipulating cloth around a stand or model of a human shape. The result enabled pattern pieces to be cut, and from these more garments could be made. From this developed the idea of basic pattern blocks which (in theory) could be used to create any style. Today, patterns can be created instantly by computer using a pattern design system (PDS). With both stored information and data that is input by the operator, the system can produce pattern pieces that automatically feature pleats, darts, fullness and seam allowances.

Grading and marking

GMS (grading and marking systems) are advanced systems that carry out **grading** and **marker planning**. Grading is the process of increasing or decreasing a pattern to produce the same outfit but in a variety of standard sizes. Measurements are fed into the computer, the new sizes are calculated and the altered pattern pieces are produced. Marker planning is the process of accurately marking the patterns so they will match when they are joined together. Features such as zips and buttons are also included.

Lay planning

A lay plan is an arrangement of pattern pieces that ensures the most economic use of fabric. A light pen is used to move the pattern pieces on the screen so waste is kept to a minimum. This information is stored and can be printed if a small-scale plan of the layout is needed.

Cutting

In mass or batch production several layers of fabric are cut at the same time to speed up the process. However, a cutting marker may be required if the fabric is to be cut using a cutting tool. This is a sheet with all the pieces marked on it, that guides the cutting tool. A computerized system can produce the cutting marker. However, fully automated cutting systems will cut layers of fabric accurately and consistently using sharp, vertical knives and with little operator intervention.

Computer control

CAM enables one person to control an entire range of manufacturing operations with a computer, so it reduces the number of staff a company needs. Also, by allowing computers to control the manufacturing process, tasks are performed in exactly the same way every time so the risk of human error is reduced.

PDP

The Product Development Partnership (PDP) consists of a group of suppliers and technology companies who have got together to improve communication in the clothing industry. As more and more companies become computerized, it is clear that different systems need to be compatible for communication purposes. For example, a stock control system may be incompatible with the supplier's ordering system. PDP aims to include the whole supply chain in a compatible system, from fabric production right through to the consumer.

Computers have speeded up clothing manufacture. ▶

production systems

Like most areas of manufacturing, the clothing industry relies heavily on production systems. These systems involve a series of activities or parts that:

- are essential to the production
- are connected in an organized way
- cause a change during the production

A production system may be thought of as a series of interconnections between materials, tasks, machines and components.

Inputs and outputs

In order for a system to exist, even in a simple form, it requires **inputs**, **outputs** and processes. The input is everything that is put into the system, so this will include materials, workers, equipment, energy etc. The output is the end-product of the system, so this may be, say, a T-shirt or skeins (large bundles) of dyed **yarn**, depending on the specific system. Clearly something must happen to the inputs in order to achieve the outputs. Anything that affects or changes the inputs is referred to as a process. A system is used to ensure outputs are produced as efficiently as possible.

Setting standards

As well as ensuring production efficiency, a system can help to maintain standards within the production process. By using a system, a task may be made easier to do or a process may become more efficient. The pace of certain processes can be adjusted when necessary and tasks can be monitored to ensure consistency. Production can be made more cost effective when using a system.

Defining the boundaries

A system may be a combination of several smaller systems known as sub-systems. The sub-systems rely on one another for the successful production of an output so if one sub-system breaks down, the overall system will be affected. For this reason it is necessary to define the system boundary or boundaries. Everything belonging to a particular boundary is part of that system. So, a boundary may be established around a particular area of production, perhaps cutting out or finishing. Then, when a system needs to be tested or adjusted, only the processes belonging to that specific system boundary will need to be analysed.

These items may be regarded ▶
as inputs into a system.

The end product of a system is known as an output. This might be an item of clothing such as a shirt.

System control

It has already been said that systems can make production more efficient but efficiency really comes into its own when the system is controlled. Today computers are commonly used to control systems in the clothing industry. Computer-aided design (CAD) and computer-aided manufacture (CAM) are the main methods of controlling the design and manufacturing stages (see pages 24–5).

Feedback

The success of a system is determined by its ability to transform its inputs into outputs. In addition to control, a system relies on feedback to ensure quality outputs are produced. Feedback is the information that is passed back along the system. If it detects a problem, changes to the system can be made straight away. There are two main types of feedback system: open feedback and closed-loop feedback.

Open feedback

A system of open feedback is used when an adjustment can be made manually during the production. If a computer detects shirts are not being sealed in their packaging correctly then this will show up on a screen. The machine operator can then make the necessary adjustments and production will not be greatly interrupted.

Closed-loop feedback

A closed-loop feedback system is one where an adjustment is made automatically. Sensors are often used to monitor and alter levels in a system. For example, a sensor can be used to detect temperatures and cause them to increase or decrease as necessary.

Just-in-time

Special systems are used to monitor stock in many areas of manufacture. In the clothing industry, the system of just-in-time means that stock such as fabric is only ordered when it is needed. The theory behind this is that if expensive stock is kept for long periods it is not actually making any money. On the other hand, it is necessary to have some items in stock all the time if they are likely to be needed. This stock system is known as just-in-case.

textiles testing

The clothing industry, as with other textile industries, must assess its products to ensure they meet the needs of the consumers for whom they were designed. Every clothing manufacturer needs to be confident that a successful product is being placed on the **market**. The assessment may involve scientific testing for garments such as waterproof, weatherproof jackets for mountaineers, or a more aesthetic judgement about some luxury clothes. The process of assessing items is carried out using various evaluation methods and may take place at any stage of design and production.

Types of evaluation

If garments are tested throughout the whole process, from design to end-product, they are being continuously evaluated. On the other hand, specific aspects may be chosen for selective evaluation – for example, testing the strength of a fastener. If garments are to be tested at the end of the process then the evaluation will be a comprehensive one, covering the whole product. However, whatever type of evaluation is used, there must be standards against which each aspect can be judged. These standards are known as **criteria**.

Some examples of criteria used when evaluating clothes are shown in the box below. The criteria for a scientific test may involve a particular set of results so it is easy to assess if the product has met the criteria. A comprehensive evaluation of a garment may be more difficult to assess against criteria because there may be conflicts in the results. If some criteria are met but others are not, a decision is made about which are most important for that particular item.

Examples of evaluation criteria

- Aesthetics – do consumers find it aesthetically pleasing?
- Cost to the environment – what will the effects be on the environment?
- Fitness for purpose – are all components able to carry out the garment's function?
- Function – does the garment perform the task it is supposed to?
- Safety – does it meet legal safety standards?
- Size – does the garment fit the consumer or meet the standard sizing?
- Special needs – do any special considerations (such as use by the disabled) need to be made?
- Value for money – can it be sold at a price consumers are prepared to pay?

Product specifications

To ensure a garment meets the needs of its consumer target group, all the criteria used to evaluate it are set out in its **product specification**. This is written during a design process, after the garment design has been thoroughly researched and tested. The fabrics and components will be specified, as well as the manufacturing processes, constraints of cost, size and time. Clearly, to evaluate a product effectively, it must be assessed against these specifications when it is completed. For example, if the production costs were actually higher than stated in the specification (perhaps due to the manufacturer being let down by a supplier) then the garment may fail to meet the cost criteria. This may then lead to the target consumer group being unwilling to pay the higher price necessary to cover the extra costs. The garment has then failed to meet two of its evaluation criteria, when checked against its product specification.

Tolerance levels

When evaluating some products it is difficult to assess them with 100 per cent accuracy. This may be because the production is very complex or the item itself is very complex. For this reason, the clothing industry regularly uses **tolerance levels** when testing certain criteria. This means that the assessment can fall within a previously set range, with an upper and a lower limit. For example, men's trousers may be labelled with a length of 112cm but during the testing procedure the trousers will be acceptable if their length falls within the range 110cm–114cm. Any measurement outside these tolerance levels would make the garment unacceptable. A tolerance level is an example of a constraint placed on a design. A constraint is something that sets limitation, either within a range, like a tolerance level, or something that is precise, like a fabric being waterproof.

evaluating textiles

Market research

A lot of clothes are highly functional while others may be practical but also have an aesthetic appeal. Functional clothes will require scientific testing but most clothes also need to be assessed by the target consumer group. This may be carried out using **market research**.

Market research involves gathering information from consumers who are from the same target group and finding out what they think about a particular item. Sometimes market research is carried out in shopping centres where there are lots of people. The researcher will ask people who appear to fit in the target group, say, males aged between eighteen and thirty. The researcher will probably have a questionnaire from which they ask questions and record the consumer's answers.

To assess whether garments meet consumer needs the market research often involves asking consumers to look at the clothes and answer questions about them. This type of research is more **subjective** because the consumer is giving a personal opinion about something. To make this information easier to assess, there may be a variety of options the consumer can choose from. The research may be in the form of a questionnaire or it could be an interview. Consumers may be on their own or part of a group. The more people included in market research, the more reliable the results are likely to be when collated and analysed.

▲ Market research plays an important role in finding out what consumers think about products.

Comparing clothes

In the early stages of a design process, similar existing products are often compared and even **disassembled** in order to develop design ideas. The aim is to produce ideas that will be an improvement on existing products.

However, even when a garment has been completed it may be useful to evaluate it against other similar garments. Comparing items is a useful exercise in market research because consumers can say what they think of a new garment when it is compared with something similar, but perhaps made using a different fabric. Garments may also be compared with or contrasted to clothes that are more expensive, to see whether the consumers are getting more value for money.

Testing garments

Scientific testing has to be carried out on many items of clothing. Functional clothes such as protective uniforms must pass stringent tests laid down by law. Finished garments will be tested at regular intervals to ensure standards are being maintained. Although this type of testing will mean the product is destroyed in the process, it is an essential part of the evaluation process.

Before a garment is launched on the market, it may go through a trial period. Either a **prototype** or the final product is worn and used for a period of time to evaluate its success. The trial may involve something as simple as giving a group of parents dungarees for their toddlers for a period of three weeks. During that time the parents have to assess the suitability of the clothes. This may include an evaluation of:
- the fastenings used
- getting the dungarees on and off
- the child's comfort and freedom of movement
- washing and drying the dungarees.

Trialling clothes in a real life situation is important to ensure they are designed and made to meet consumer needs.

This sort of trialling is particularly useful for clothes that need to be practical, such as uniforms and work clothes. Someone trialling the outfit can say whether the pockets are in the right place and whether they are large enough to hold all the necessary tools and equipment. It must be remembered, though, that it is impossible to please everyone all the time, so the more people involved in the trialling, the easier the results will be to analyse.

Reviewing the system
Even when a product has been made and the outcome is successful, it is good working practice for a review to take place. This can involve reviewing all stages in the design and manufacturing process. It may be that a manufacturing technique has been used for the first time and, even though it may have worked well during the production of a prototype, there are aspects that can be refined and improved. Equally, the process may work so well that its review will enable the manufacturer to use it in other production areas.

textile quality

Consumer quality

The term 'quality' can be defined as a level of excellence. But what may be regarded as excellent by one consumer may not be considered excellent by another. Consumers are likely to judge the quality of clothes in a number of ways, depending on the item. Football shorts, for example, must be hard-wearing, fit properly and be reasonably priced. However, an outfit for a special occasion may be judged on its aesthetic qualities, or what it looks like, rather than its performance. Consumers may also place importance on value for money or price, depending on the garment and what they can afford.

Industrial quality

The clothing industry also defines quality in terms of levels of excellence. However, their judgements must be based on **objective** measurements rather than **subjective** ones. Testing is necessary in order to ensure quality outcomes are produced. A company needs a good reputation and loyalty from its consumers and it can only achieve this if it is producing products of a consistently high standard.

Quality has to be assessed throughout the entire process, not just at the end of production, and the assessments must take into account the **product specification**. Quality of design and quality of manufacture are separate

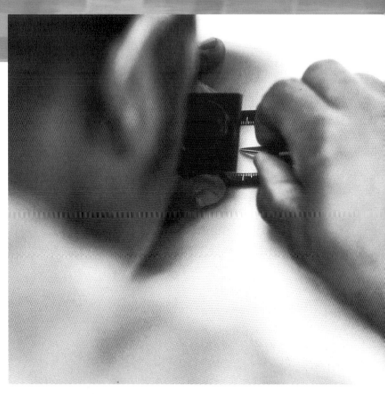

▲ Testing in the clothing industry is essential if quality outcomes are to be produced.

aspects but they are dependent on one another in the production of a quality item of clothing. Quality is assessed using quality assurance, quality control and attribute analysis.

Quality assurance

Quality assurance is an overall approach to quality. It ensures standards are maintained because checks are made at every stage, from design to packaging. This gives the consumer the satisfaction of knowing that the company is giving its assurance that standards have been met. Quality assurance relies on everyone in the production process achieving the targets set for their area of work. By giving all workers responsibility in this way, they are more likely to take pride in what they do and that helps the business to run more efficiently. This system is known as Total Quality Management.

Quality control

Most companies have one or more quality controllers who are in charge of quality control. This is a method of ensuring and maintaining quality at every stage of production. It includes checking the raw materials and **components**, all steps of production and the final outcome. The quality controller checks that the product is within its **tolerance level**. However, quality control is not just a system of checks. It is also about ensuring everyone involved knows exactly what to do and how to do it. Instructions for workers must be clear and training given if necessary.

Quality control checks ensure that the product specification is being met. It may include details such as the size of stitches or the type of button. If these do not match the specification, the garment has to be rejected or altered which leads to a loss of time and money.

Attribute analysis

Another method of ensuring quality products are produced is known as attribute analysis. This involves checking products to see whether or not they have any defects. During the manufacture visual checks are made to see that garments have been assembled in the right way and that the stitching is correct. When attribute analysis is used in mass production, the quality can be assessed mathematically by working out the percentage of faulty goods produced. The smaller the percentage, the better the quality of production.

Quality signs

It is important for both consumers and the clothing industry that products are labelled to show the standard of the goods. Various quality signs used on textile items are shown here, although there are others that are used on garments. For example, flame retardant clothing can display the quality sign mark CEN if the fabric has fire retardant properties that meet European Union specifications.

The Woolmark Company lays down standards of quality and performance and only items which meet these standards are allowed to carry the Woolmark. Other examples of quality symbols include the Woolmark Blend, The Wool Blend, the International Cotton Emblem, the Irish Linen trademark and the Silk Seal.

 Examples of quality symbols that can be found on textile items.

33

consumer protection

Even with rigorous procedures of quality testing in place, it is possible that faulty garments may reach the consumer. In order to protect the consumer against unscrupulous manufacturers who could otherwise get away with selling substandard goods, a number of acts of law have been established.

Consumer Protection Act 1987

This act of law makes it an offence for anyone to put misleading prices on their goods. For example, if a rail of jumpers states '£19.99 or below' and a consumer chooses a jumper and is charged £25.99, then the sign has been misleading. In this case the consumer has the right to complain. This act also covers sales and special offers.

Consumer Credit Act 1974

This act provides protection for consumers who purchase goods using credit. It is aimed at credit companies rather than retailers or manufacturers.

Sale of Goods Act 1979

This act is designed to protect a consumer if faulty goods are purchased, but it also helps to prevent poor quality goods being sold in the first place. The act says:

- Goods must be of merchantable quality, e.g. if a pair of boots are worn once and the heel falls off, they cannot be regarded as good quality.
- Goods must be as described, e.g. a jacket described as 'leather' must not actually be made from a manufactured fabric.

- Goods must be fit for the purpose for which they are to be used, e.g. if a raincoat states 'waterproof' then it must not let in rain.

Trade Descriptions Act 1968

This act makes it an offence to describe goods (or services) incorrectly. For example, if a garment's care label states it can be washed at 60°C, and the garment shrinks when it is washed at that temperature, the consumer can take it back to the retailer. This act also applies to spoken descriptions so retailers must take care to answer consumers' questions correctly.

Consumer organizations

There are now a number of organizations whose role it is to help protect consumers. These organizations include:
- Citizens' Advice Bureaux (CAB)
- Office of Fair Trading (OFT)
- **British Standards Institute** (BSI)
- Consumers Association (CA), (publishers of *Which?* magazine)
- Local Authority Trading Standards Officer and Consumer Protection Departments.

In addition, consumers can get a great deal of help from the media. Television programmes such as *Watchdog* and *You and Yours* on the radio publicize information about faulty goods or poor service received by consumers.

Care labels

Nearly all garments carry care labels giving information about their fibre

Examples of some care labels. ▶

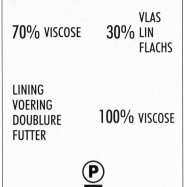

content, cleaning instructions and any other relevant information. If a label cannot actually be attached to the clothing, on socks for example, it is likely to be provided on the packaging. Examples of some care labels and the details they carry are shown here.

HLCC

In order to ensure all manufacturers use the same **criteria** when applying care labels to their textile items, the Home Laundering and Consultative Council has developed an International Textile Care Labelling Scheme. The scheme involves a set of symbols or codes to cover all aspects of laundering textile products. It is called the International Care Labelling Code and examples of its symbols and what they mean are shown on the right.

Safety labels

As well as having care labels, many items of clothing must be labelled by law to give the consumer information about any risks from fire. Flammability warnings must appear on nightwear and they may include expressions such as 'Carelessness causes fire', 'Warning. Keep away from fire' or 'Low flammability'. The British Standards Institute have set various standards of flammability which are recognized by a BS number. These may be quoted on a label like this, 'Low flammability to BS 5722'.

▼ *Symbols from the International Care Labelling Code.*

the jeans success story

Levi Strauss & Co.

Levi Strauss are one of the world's largest brandname clothing companies. They manufacture and market jeans and casual sportswear using the following brand names; Levis®, Dockers® and Slates®. The company has registered the Levis® trademark in more than 200 countries.

Levis Strauss & Co. employ approximately 1600 staff at their San Francisco headquarters and another 30,000 people worldwide. They have 32 production facilities and 29 customer service centres throughout the world.

Levi history

Levi Strauss was a Bavarian immigrant who went to San Francisco in 1853. When he first arrived he was told he would need some hardwearing trousers, so he made some for himself out of canvas. This could be said to be the first pair of Levi jeans! Over the next twenty years he built up a very successful business selling dry goods and manufacturing work clothes which included 'waist overalls' that we know today as jeans.

When miners began to complain of torn pockets caused by the heavy gold nuggets they carried, Levi Strauss decided to develop a method of reinforcing the pockets. He enlisted the help of a tailor called Jacob W. Davis who came up with the idea of using a copper wire to rivet the pockets. The rivet was **patented** in 1873 and this was the start of rivets so familiar on today's jeans.

▲ The ever-popular Levi jeans.

When Levis Strauss died in 1902 he left his thriving business to his four nephews. The family continue to control it today.

Levi's® 501®

Levi's® 501® jeans were first created in the 1800s and were given the number 501 around 1890. They are distinguished by their button-fly and their Shrink-To-Fit® nature. They are the oldest and best selling product of Levi Strauss & Co. They are made from serge de Nimes denim, a type of cotton twill originally made in Nimes, France, over 500 years ago. The denim is dyed blue with indigo (see opposite). In 1936 the Red Tab Device® was created to help identify Levi's® 501® jeans from a distance. These jeans were called waist overalls up until 1960.

Today Levi's® 501® jeans are made in approximately 108 sizes with 20 different finishes and fabrics. The typical production for one pair requires $1\frac{3}{4}$ yards of denim and 213 yards of thread.

In addition it has five buttons and five rivets. Thirty-seven separate sewing operations are involved in the making of a single pair of Levi's® 501® jeans.

Cutting and stitching

A roll of denim cloth is referred to as a bolt and each one weighs about a quarter of a tonne. The cloth is cut using an electric saw which slices through 120 layers at one time. One bolt of denim can be used to cut about 60 pairs of jeans.

Jeans are well known for their double row of stitching on the back pockets and inside legs. Today this double stitching is called Arcuate Design® and it is one of the oldest trademarks used in clothing manufacture. It was first used in 1873 and was so popular that during the Second World War, stitches were painted on back pockets because rationing meant thread was in short supply.

Rivets

In the early days of jeans making, rivets were placed on both front and back pockets. As the wearing of jeans became more widespread in America there were complaints that the rivets on the back pockets were scratching school chairs and horses' saddles. In 1937 this problem was initially solved by covering the rear rivets. However, since 1967 back pocket rivets have been replaced altogether with reinforced stitching.

Indigo blue

Traditionally the woad plant (*Isatis tinctoria*) produces the blue colour called indigo that is used to dye denim, although a synthetic version was developed in the late 1800s. Recently the Ministry of Agriculture and several companies have funded a research project into the development of a new crop of woad to produce natural indigo. Gorham & Batesman (Agriculture) Ltd, based in Norfolk, are one of the Woad Project partners. They have been trialling the pilot crop, which can produce blue dye in just twelve minutes. India and China supply most of the natural dye to Britain but growing consumer demand for natural processes and sources should mean the project will be profitable.

textile project: denim

For this project, you will be producing a portfolio. A portfolio is a collection of ideas presented together. If you wish to go on and make one or more items from your collection then this will extend your experience of working with textiles. You could develop your own pattern from your sketches or you could use a commercial pattern that may, or may not, need to be adapted.

Denim range

This project involves creating a new range of denim clothing. The range could be for yourself, or for a particular group of consumers such as toddlers. Or it could be a particular type of clothing such as sports or casual wear. Another alternative would be to design a range from one item of clothing, for example, a range of shirts, or a new range of jeans. Keep

your **target consumer group** in mind all the time you are designing.

Read through the following information before you start your designs but remember you can sketch rough ideas at any time, whenever you feel inspired.

Inspired by denim

Jeans provide a famous and lasting example of workwear that has moved into the area of fashion. Following the popularity of jeans as an item of clothing for men, women and children alike, other textile items have branched into denim. Denim is now regularly used for many types of clothing as well as accessories and household furnishings.

Denim can be worn in a variety of situations from casual wear to workwear.

38

Apart from blue, denim is now available in a range of colours and in different weights or thicknesses. Variations include denim that is faded or patterned, stretch denim and patchwork denim. In addition to jeans, clothes that can be made using denim include shorts, shirts, waistcoats, hats, shoes, dresses and skirts. Denim is a 'universal' fabric suitable for all ages and both genders.

Researching the fabric

It is a good idea to research a fabric thoroughly before starting to produce design ideas. However, this does not have to be hard work. Research can involve looking at clothes shops to see what is already available in denim or a visit to a fabric shop. If you do not intend to make the garments you could design your own style of denim that perhaps isn't available in shops.

What's around?

Research also involves keeping your eyes open to everything around you. What are other people wearing in the street? On the television? In magazines? Look at your own denim clothes. What style are they? Do they have features that are special to denim such as top stitching, metal buttons, studs, rivets, contrasting thread? Will you use any of these techniques or will you move away from anything usually associated with denim?

Make sure you record any important research in the form of sketches, notes, swatches of fabric, magazine cuttings etc.

Presenting ideas

Look carefully at your research before starting work on your portfolio of ideas. Also, decide how you wish to present your ideas and what you will show them on. You could use a sketch pad or you could present them on one large display board perhaps as a **mood board**. The clothes should be sketched in pencil and then either coloured in or samples of colour created around each labelled drawing. Your sketches can be enhanced with swatches of fabric, fastenings, even notes about construction techniques if you wish.

One way to present your design ideas might be in the form of a 'denim book'. Decorate a piece of A3 card with some denim fabric and then fold it in half to form the sleeve of an A4 book. The clothing designs could be presented on white A4 paper or card with perhaps a corner covered in denim to give a consistent denim feel throughout. The A4 design sheets can then be slipped inside the denim sleeve. Presentation is very important with fashion design so plan this carefully before you begin.

Clothes can be displayed on their own or on models. If you find it difficult to draw people an outline can be traced so each model is the same every time.

Building a range of portfolios such as this one can help to develop both design and making skills because it is important to understand how garments are made in order to design them successfully.

finishing techniques

The way clothes are treated by the consumer is largely dependent on the method of their construction and fibre content. A non-woven fabric like felt will not withstand a machine wash whereas a fabric made from 100 per cent cotton will wash well but will also need ironing. However, the properties of fabric can be altered or enhanced with the application of special finishing techniques.

Finishing techniques are usually permanent and so will last the lifetime of the garment. However, some clothes have a temporary finish that will be lost after the fabric is cleaned. Other finishes are renewable and can be reapplied, in the same way leather shoes can be sprayed to protect them against the rain.

Physical finishes

These finishes are applied mechanically and result in a change in the fabric's appearance and/or texture. They include calendering, filling, raising and tentering.

- Calendering – produces fabric with a smooth surface and silky lustre. **Chintz** is an example of a plain weave cotton that has been calendered. The process is relatively straightforward as it involves fabric being passed between heated rollers. The rollers can be engraved to produce a fabric with an embossed pattern. Eventually this finish will wear off.
- Filling – used to make a loosely woven cheap fabric appear smooth and strong by soaking it in a starch solution. The fabric then goes through the calendering process. This finish will only last until the starch is rinsed away in the first wash.

▲ A waterproof finish is essential for rainwear.

- Raising – an example of a permanent finishing technique. The fabric passes through a series of rollers covered in wire which gently tease out the fibre ends from the weave. The technique must be carried out gently otherwise the fibres would tear and weaken the fabric. The result is a raised surface and a fluffy texture. Such fabrics can be used for winter clothes that help to keep the wearer warm.
- Tentering – applied to fabrics that have lost their shape during the construction process. In order to restore the shape, the fabric is dipped in a chemical bath, then it travels through a machine which grips the **selvedges** with tiny clips. The machine holds the fabric while it is heat dried, and the finished fabric returns to its correct shape. Tentering does not have a permanent effect so the fabric may shrink again once it has been washed.

Chemical finishes

Unlike physical finishes, a chemical finish can be applied at any point during the production process, from fibre to fabric. Some examples are given here.

- Flameproofing finishes – applied to **yarns** and fabrics. Items such as soft furnishings and children's nightwear have to be produced according to strict guidelines laid down by the **British Standards Institute**. Such items must also be clearly labelled because the flammability protection may be lost if they are washed incorrectly.
- Crease-resistant finishes (permanent) – reduce the need for ironing. Fabrics that crease easily, and therefore are likely to be given this treatment, include cotton, linen and viscose. A resin is applied to the fabric which is then dried and heat-set.
- Stain- and dirt-resistant finishes – used on furnishing fabrics and curtains. Sometimes manufacturers provide this as an optional extra when selling sofas, armchairs and sofabeds. The finish works by providing a barrier over the fibres preventing dirt and grease from penetrating the fabric.
- Shrink-resistant finishes – often applied to wool fibres as they are most likely to shrink. The chemicals used prevent the scales on the wool fibres from interlocking which causes **felting** when the wool is washed. The finish may be applied to the fibre or after the item has been fully constructed. It is due to this finish that you now see 'machine washable' labels on wool garments.

- Waterproofing finishes – used on items such as raincoats, jackets, umbrellas and hats. The chemicals involved, usually silicone, prevent water from soaking into the fabric yet still allow air to pass through. However, once the fabric becomes **saturated**, water will soak through it.

Wonder Wash fabric

A textile company in India have developed a fabric that does not require detergent to get rid of stains such as tea, coffee, curry and tomato sauce. The Wonder Wash fabric is treated with a special chemical that allows water vapour to pass through by molecular action. This treatment causes a breathable membrane to form so the fabric does not need detergent or soap when it is washed. Wonder Wash fabric is simply put in warm water for 35 minutes, then rinsed and dried. If the stain is particularly stubborn then only 15–20 per cent of the normal detergent is required and this is applied directly on to the stain. Perhaps one day washing clothes will be a thing of the past!

careers in the clothing industry

This unit describes some of the main types of employment within the clothing industry. Like most areas of manufacturing, the employment structure will vary from company to company, and a variety of other jobs are also likely to be available.

Retail buyer

Clothes are usually sold by retailers. The retailer supplies products according to the consumer demand. It is the responsibility of the retail buyer to anticipate the needs of the **market**. This rather difficult task involves estimating what consumers are likely to buy and in what quantity. The buyer orders the goods from the manufacturer and decides their **price bracket**. In a small business, the buying may be carried out by the owner. A large company may employ several buyers who specialize in a particular area such as accessories or children's wear.

Fashion designer

Today, a designer needs to have knowledge of all aspects of clothing production. This gives him or her the ability to anticipate which styles and construction techniques can be used in mass production. A designer must be able to produce sketches that are drawn to scale. These differ from fashion drawings, where the body is often **elongated**. Designers produce working drawings which contain all the information needed for a pattern to be made. Computer-aided design (CAD) packages are also used by many designers today (see page 24).

Pattern cutter

Pattern cutters are considered by many to be the most important technicians in the whole process of garment manufacture. They fall into two categories – those that work in the design department to produce **prototype** paper patterns and those that produce the final production pattern made from card, plastic or metal.

Textile designer

The emphasis on fibre technology in the clothing industry has increased in recent years, and so has the importance of the textile designer. These designers may work in conjunction with a fashion designer. Together they can anticipate the market, in terms of style and fabric. They are creative people who may have a background in textile science.

A background in textile science is useful for a career in textile design. ▶

A sample machinist. ▶

Sample machinist

The sample machinist is responsible for making up a garment and assessing whether it is possible to mass produce it. The amount of time it will take and the costs involved also have to be considered. A sample machinist will be experienced enough to estimate the most logical order for garment assembly. An in-house model will try on the sample garment so it can be adjusted if necessary.

Cutting room manager

The cutting room is where all fabric cutting takes place. Depending on the size and type of company, different types of machine and numbers of people are employed to do the cutting. The manager of the cutting room has to oversee all processes and is responsible for the quality of the cutting. The manager must also ensure the cut pieces are passed on to the production area at the correct time.

Assembly machinists

There are many types of assembly systems in use today (see pages 26–27). Technology is becoming more and more advanced, but basically garments may be constructed in two ways. A machinist may be given all the **component** parts and is responsible for the garments from start to finish. This method is usually used by small companies. Alternatively, garments may be produced using a **production line** assembly where a machinist will be responsible for one aspect of the construction. Special machine operators are trained to finish garments by using **overlockers**, buttonhole and button-sewing machines, multi-needle machines and so on.

The presser

Another specialized area of garment construction is the pressing of clothes. Some pressing is essential during assembly because it cannot be done properly when the garment is complete. This is usually done using a hand iron. The final finishing press may be done by hand or machine, using specialized steam and vacuum presses, or a mixture of both. Trained operators are required to carry out the pressing.

Warehouse manager

All completed garments or **stock** are kept in warehouses. It is the job of the warehouse manager to organize the stock ready for dispatch to the retailer. This may involve using a computerized system of stock control.

resources

Books

The following books are useful for students studying GCSE Design and Technology:

Design & Make It! Textiles Technology Alex McArthur, Carolyn Etchells, Tristram Shepard	Stanley Thornes 1997
Examining Textiles Technology Anne Barnett	Heinemann Educational 1997
Textiles and Technology (UK edition) Adapted by Margaret Beith	Cambridge University Press 1997
Textiles Technology Alison Bartle and Bernie O'Connor	Causeway Press 1997

The following books are useful for more detailed information on the clothing industry:

CAD in Clothing and Textiles (2nd edition) Edited by Winifred Aldrich	Blackwell Scientific Publications 1994
Fashion Design and Product Development Harold Carr and John Pomeroy	Blackwell Science Ltd 1992
The Technology of Clothing Manufacture (2nd edition) Harold Carr and Barbara Latham	Blackwell Science Ltd 1994

I.C.T.

www.craftscouncil.org.uk/exhib.htm
Provides details of forthcoming arts and crafts events throughout the country

www.levistrauss.com
To find out more about Levi jeans

www.textile-toolkit.org.uk
Includes news, competitions, details of events and a chat forum for students; there is also a CD-ROM available for use as a teaching aid for GCSE textiles

www.worldtextile.com
Publishes a variety of textile-related journals

Places to visit

Luton Museum and Art Gallery
Wardown Park
Luton LU2 7HA
(Tel no: 01582 546722)
*This museum provides comprehensive
information about the hat industry*

Contacts

The Crafts Council
44a Pentonville Road
London NI 9BY
(Tel no: 020 7278 7700)
*Provides up-to-date information about
art and crafts exhibitions and shows; also
produces a magazine called* Crafts,
available on subscription

Journals

World Clothing Manufacturer
World Textile Publications Ltd
Perkin House
1 Longlands Street
Bradford
West Yorkshire BD1 2TP
(Tel no: 01274 378800)
*A magazine written for the clothing
industry worldwide*

glossary

backlatch machine is an overlock machine with an attachment at the front which automatically catches the loose thread from one lot of stitching so it is ready to start the next stitching

bespoke describes clothes that are custom-made by a tailor

British Standards Institute professional organization which decides which tests must be applied to which textile products, and sets the standards for the tests

chintz glazed or shiny fabric, often made of cotton and used mainly for furnishings

client person or company for whom designer is producing a design or range of designs

component part of a garment prior to assembly including accessories

couture short for 'haute couture' (see below)

criteria standards of judgement that are used, for example, in evaluating the quality of textile products

disassemble take apart a garment or textile item in order to find out more about its construction

elongate make something extra long; for example the legs of models in fashion drawings are usually drawn disproportionately long

fad a short-lived fashion

felting matting effect that occurs when fabric, especially wool, is washed at too high a temperature, or too vigorously

garment performance extent to which a garment meets performance standards such as being waterproof or having good stretch recovery

grading producing pattern pieces in a range of sizes

haute couture French term meaning high-quality clothes, designed and made for a very limited market

house the fashion industry's term for 'company'

input everything that is put into the production system, including materials, workers, equipment and energy

labour-intensive involving a lot of work and taking a lot of time

marker planning process of accurately marking the patterns so they will match when they are joined together

market consumers, or a particular sector of consumers

marketing all activities involved in getting garments to consumers; for example selling, advertising, promoting

market research research carried out to find out what consumers think about existing products or about new products, or to find out about their needs

mass market consumers, on a large scale

milliner a person who makes hats

mood board display board covered with pictures, sketches, swatches (samples of material) etc., used to create a mood or feeling about a product to be designed; often used when talking to the target consumer group; also known as a 'theme board'

objective something that depends on facts rather than a person's point of view

output end-product of manufacture; for example a finished garment

outside contractor company which takes on work for another company, either because it is a specialist task or to help during times of excessive workload

overlocker machine that will simultaneously stitch, trim and neaten seams

patent owning the sole right to a new product or process; it has to be applied for

perceived consumer need result of market research; what researchers believe consumers want

price bracket a price range given to items of clothing that have been categorized

product development process of producing and developing new ideas in order to improve on a product or to create a new one

production line production carried out on a garment or product, one process at a time, by different workers

product specification precise details about a particular product – such as type of fabric and size of stitches, relevant manufacturing processes, constraints of cost, size and time – so that it can be reproduced on a large scale

promote publicize something in order to sell it

prototype model of a design idea, used to test its suitability for production

saturate make completely wet

selvedges firm area of fabric created by strong warp threads (threads running vertically) running along the edges of the fabric

stock all items available for sale by a retailer or manufacturer

subjective something that depends on a person's point of view or opinion rather than on fact

suburban residential area that is on the outskirts of a town or city

target consumer group group of consumers such as the elderly, teenagers, or sportswomen being targeted for a product because they are the ones most likely to buy it

toile garment modelled in calico or similar fabric during prototype stage

tolerance level in evaluating a garment, a set range of acceptability, with an upper and a lower limit, that must be met; for example when the specification on trouser length is 112cm, the tolerance level may be 110cm–114cm

yarn single strand of fibres that have been spun together

index